#RU Hooked

TEENS & SOCIAL MEDIA

*To my loving wife, Heather. She is my partner in ministry,
the mother of our children, and my best friend.*

*Thanks, Babe, for not being selfish with
my time and your devotion, not only to me
but also to our Savior. I love you!*

J S

Library of Congress Cataloging-in-Publication Data

Names: Smith, Jonathan, 1977 October 24- author.
Title: #RUHooked / written by Jonathan Smith.
Description: Minneapolis : TRISTAN Publishing, [2017] | Audience:
    Grade 9 to 12. | Audience: Age: 12-18.
Identifiers: LCCN 2017025644 | ISBN 9781939881175 (alk. paper)
Subjects: LCSH: Technology and youth--Juvenile literature. | Information
    society--Social aspects--Juvenile literature. | Social media—
    Juvenile literature.
Classification: LCC HQ784.T37 S65 2017 | DDC 303.48/33--dc23
LC record available at https://lccn.loc.gov/2017025644

TRISTAN Publishing, Inc.
2355 Louisiana Avenue North
Golden Valley, MN 55427

To learn about all of our books with a message, please visit
www.TRISTANpublishing.com

#RU Hooked

ENS & SOCIAL MED

FOR TEENS AND
THE PEOPLE WHO
CARE ABOUT THEM

JONATHAN SMITH

PART ONE

Society, Social Media, & You

You love social media. You enjoy checking up on your friends and staying current on the latest memes. You're thrilled when a new social media site comes online, and you're anxious to be among the first to try it out and reserve your same username. You know what? That's okay. You're not alone.

Technology is a vital aspect of our lives. It is how we connect with our friends and listen to music. It is how we express our personalities and how we make our likes and dislikes known—not just to our friends, but also to the world. In many ways, your use of social media controls the world. If adults want to know what the next big trend in technology or social media is, then they need to look no farther than where the teenagers are. That's incredible to think about, and it shows how much control you have just by the networks you use. Where will you go next—and why?

You are among the most connected group of people in the world. All the studies basically say the same thing, that almost all of you have smart devices and spend time online. There are just differing degrees of how often you're online.

What are you doing when you're online? Checking social media. **Social media is the number one activity for all internet users worldwide.** Even adults check social media more often than they check the news, their bank accounts, or the weather. Think about your friends for a minute. Do you have friends who are online constantly? What about several times per day? What about you? What about me?

WHAT ARE YOU DOING WHEN YOU'RE ONLINE?

When we talk about "social media," we aren't just talking about the sites and platforms themselves. We are also talking about the content placed on those sites, as well as the technology used to connect to those sites. The picture you took, the smartphone or tablet you used, the caption you wrote, and the platform you posted it to are all part of social media.

I am an active and avid social media user. I have an account on most social media sites. Making the right connections online and interacting in the right way have definitely given me some very cool opportunities. Using social media, I've gotten access to secured government facilities at NASA, even sitting close enough to get singed at numerous rocket launches; and I've visited the White House several times, among other things. I would never have thought that a social media site would lead to meeting the President of the United States. I'm definitely pro-social media, and I encourage others to use it as well. I embrace new technology when it comes out, and I'm always looking ahead to the next big thing. Many times, I'm looking at you for guidance on what's next and how to use it!

Your parents struggle to keep up with you and how quickly you learn and use new technology. You can start a Netflix movie on their TV from your phone—from across town—before your parents have even found the remote control. Adults depend on you to help them learn the latest features on their smartphones and how to post a picture to Facebook. Without you, your parents' DVR might sit empty.

I know the last thing you need is another long reading assignment. It is my hope and prayer for you—as you engage with this little book—that first, you desire to grow and mature in your use of social media, and also that you want to use it responsibly with accountability. Second, **in order to accomplish responsible social media use with accountability, I hope you recognize your need for help and that you can't**

do it alone. Yes, your parents have a role to play here, but you also have a role in your relationship with Jesus Christ. Without Him, your goals may be admirable, but your success will be limited.

If you desire to use social media and technology in a responsible way that pleases God, then please keep reading.

As you read, you will see a lot of mentions referring to your parents. I understand that some of you might not even live with your parents. That's fine. Just remember that when I refer to your parents, it can also mean any authority figure where you live—whether your grandparents, other relatives, foster parents, a friend's family, or the adults in charge of your living situation. For our purposes, the word *parents* covers all of the above.

PART TWO

Are You Hooked?

Before you say you don't have a problem, **ask yourself these questions:**

1. Do you ever walk and post from your device at the same time?

2. Do you use your device while driving, without using a hands-free connection?

3. Does your anxiety rise when you are separated from your device?

4. Do you get nervous wondering what others are posting about you?

5. Do you get concerned that there are activities taking place without you?

6. Do you argue with people online?

7. Have any of those arguments ever spilled out into the real world?

8. Are you slow to obey when asked to give up your device?

9. Have you ever taken a compromising photo of someone—or had a compromising photo taken of you?

10. Would you rather spend time with your device instead of your family and friends?

11. Do you check your device often when you should be paying attention to a movie or church service or concert or TV show or class?

12. Do you have fake accounts that you only show your parents—or accounts that you don't show them at all?

13. Do you want to stop reading this?

How many questions did you answer with "yes"? Just because you don't think you have a problem doesn't mean you don't. **The more "yes" answers you had, the more likely it is that you are prioritizing your device and social media connections over other priorities in your life.**

Are you sure you don't have a problem?

Many teenagers consider themselves addicted to social media. One study found that many young people check their social media accounts over 100 times per day. How many times do you check your account? Keep track one day. I think the results will surprise you.

One popular activity—for not only teens, but adults too—is lurking. Lurking is checking out whatever others are doing online, while not participating online yourself. Keeping tabs on your friends without them knowing you are monitoring them. Why lurk? Lurking comes out of the anxiety that's created when wondering what others are saying about you. This anxiety is manifested several ways. A CNN Special Report included several teens' comments.

"I would rather not eat for a week than get my phone taken away. It's really bad," said Gia, a 13-year-old. "I literally feel like I'm going to die."

"When I get my phone taken away, I feel kind of naked," said Kyla, another 13-year-old. "I do feel kind of empty without my phone." Have you ever felt this way?

It has been found that separation from our technology and online connections contributes to this anxiety. Why does this make us anxious? Oftentimes it's a concern for what others are thinking about us. Social media becomes our measure of popularity—and when we believe our popularity is dropping, we start to defend ourselves.

We know this because of the CNN study of over 150,000 posts made by more than 200 teenagers. In the study, 61% of teens said they wanted to see if their online posts were getting likes and comments. Also, 36% said they wanted to see if their friends were doing things without them. In addition, 21% said they wanted to make sure no one was saying mean things about them.

HAVE
YOU EVER
FELT THIS
WAY?

If you don't think you're part of these stats, then let me encourage you to review your social media activity over the last five days. What did you post online and why? What did you read online and why? Is your approach to social media, "If they're talking about me, then I'm going to talk about them"?

This seems to hold up when you look at the news. In January of 2013, a 16-year-old girl from central Indiana drove 60 miles to beat up a 17-year-old girl who had been spreading rumors about her on Facebook.

Even public schools are recognizing that there is value in monitoring what you post online. A public school district in California hired a private firm to follow their students online to help them predict which kids would be troublemakers in school. Of course, this was quickly shut down by a flurry of privacy lawsuits, but a stunning correlation was made: those who were trouble online were also trouble in the real world.

Cyber bullying is a real thing, just as much as bullying is in the real world. Oftentimes bullying is excused as a joke—but it's no joke, whether online or in the real world. Bullying often comes as a result of private information shared between friends that becomes instantly public when posted online.

The same is true with pictures. The old saying that a picture is worth a thousand words certainly rings true of social media. Social media sites like Twitter and Facebook started out as primarily text sites. Today they have evolved into forms of communication with pictures and images posted more often than text. This transition to pictures is empowering new apps and sites that allow for easy and secure sharing and editing of images.

The desire to be popular often leads to disclosing information we normally wouldn't tell anyone, or allowing a picture to be taken that we would never want shared. Once taken, it can't be untaken. In your parents' day, a picture could be physically destroyed. The negatives could be burned, and that image would never be able to be reproduced.

Today we can't call a social media platform and ask them to delete all the copies of our posts. Once captured in a digital format, it lives forever. Think about that.

Forever is a very long time.

Trust me, even if we are using a platform that auto-deletes, it is never really gone. We are trusting the software programmers to totally delete our messages without making a backup anywhere—and delete them in a fashion that makes them unrecoverable. Placing our trust in man for this is trust misplaced.

There is no guarantee that our message or picture can't be captured in another fashion, by another device taking a picture of the device displaying our message, as an example. There is no guarantee that the software has been written to do what they say it will do in terms of permanently deleting our messages or pictures . . . and we have no way to prove it.

Do you want to risk an image staying with you for the rest of your life? Or at the very least, know that it exists and that you live under the threat of it being released at any time? What if it comes up at a job interview? Or when you're planning to get engaged?

While there is some communication between individuals that doesn't need to be made public, if you're honoring Christ with how you use social media sites—then if your device is ever compromised, you'll have no reason to be ashamed.

If you're hiding behind platforms that pride themselves on deleting your messages to avoid getting caught, though, remember: being sinful isn't pleasing to Christ, and He already knows. You can't hide from Him.

DO YOU WANT TO RISK AN IMAGE STAYING WITH YOU FOR THE REST OF YOUR LIFE?

Rebelling (more on that later) in this fashion, aside from not honoring Christ, will not bring His blessings on your life.

The Bible says in Numbers 32:23, "But if you fail to keep your word, then you will have sinned against the Lord, and you may be sure that your sin will find you out."

We often take that literally—that if we sin, we will be found out right away—but the Bible doesn't give a timeline here. It just says that our sin will find us out. It may be quick, or it may take months (or even years!), or it may not happen in this life at all. When someone sins against us, we often wish that it would happen with our knowledge for some sort of vengeful satisfaction, but that isn't what this verse means. It means that God knows and that we will be judged, whether on this earth or after our life on this earth is over.

Of all the things that God will judge when I stand before Him, I certainly don't want my social media posts to be one of them!

I'm often asked if all this is avoidable. I don't think so. We can't avoid social media any more than we can avoid a drunk driver on the road. Totally giving up all of our technology and connectivity would be just as hard as never riding in a car. We can't just run away. Social media is here—and it is here to stay. To keep as safe as possible in a car, we must drive defensively, always with our attention focused on the road and other drivers around us. The same is true online. **To guard your heart and mind, your attention must be up, your focus must be on what is going on around you, and your goal must be to please Christ.**

While your parents may not know the difference between a smartphone and a dumb phone, **there is hope in knowing that the Bible is sufficient for all of life.** Despite the fact that the Bible was written over 2000 years ago, while the Holy Spirit was inspiring the authors of the Bible, He knew about the technology that would be available now—and even 100 years from now. As a result, we all don't have to be experts in all aspects of technology to use it properly; rather, **we have to know how to apply biblical principles to life—be it life with technology or any other aspect of living a life to serve our Savior.**

Before we can really address any struggles in life, the first thing we have to address is our relationship with our Savior. If you know that you know that you know that you believe that Jesus died and rose again on the third day to pay the price for your sins, then you have Him to fall back on for help. If you haven't decided yet whether or not you believe in the price Jesus paid for your sin, then let me encourage you to think about that now. Forever is a long time—it is a long time for that inappropriate picture of you to exist online, and it is a long time to live in a real place called hell, separated from God. Only by placing your trust in what Jesus did on the cross can you claim the free gift of eternal life, living forever with Jesus in heaven.

Otherwise, it is possible to live a good life. It is possible to do good online, but the end result is still an eternity of separation and living the rest of your life on earth without His help. If you are struggling with that decision, let me encourage you that there is nothing more important than getting this issue addressed.

If Jesus is on the throne of your heart, then you have the power of the Holy Spirit to help you grow and change to become more like Christ. The Bible says that our actions stem from what is going on in our hearts. If Jesus is on the throne of your heart, then He is there to help with any struggles in life, whether it is relationships, difficulty getting along with your parents, **or even social media.**

So what draws us to spend so much time on social media?

// PRIDE

One of the biggest draws is pride. The desire to be seen, noticed, made known, and approved. Check out my music. Check out my friends.

Check out my happenings. All of these can be quickly broadcast and shared with the masses.

Proverbs 16:18 says, "Pride goes before destruction, and haughtiness before a fall."

Also, 2 Peter 2:18–19 says, "They brag about themselves with empty, foolish boasting. With an appeal to twisted sexual desires, they lure back into sin those who have barely escaped from a lifestyle of deception. They promise freedom, but they themselves are slaves of sin and corruption. For you are a slave to whatever controls you."

Have you allowed social media to control you?

Can pride in the virtual world lead to a fall in the real world? Have you become a slave to social media? Are you helping others escape that slavery, or are you pulling them farther into it?

// POPULARITY

Pride then leads to popularity—something that's a struggle for everyone. If we're not popular in the real world, we can be popular online. We can be whatever to whomever online, and never have to worry about appearances and other pressures in the physical realm. I don't know about you, but my avatar looks a lot better than I do in person. And yes, my profile pic is an actual picture of me—and not of my dog.

Knowing we can never be popular in the physical realm can drive us to thrive online. This often leads to hacking and other disruptive online behavior that garners anonymous attention to the act. For example, one teenager released a computer virus that wreaked havoc on networks around the world. A bounty was put on the hacker's head, and eventually he was found and convicted of the crime. He wasn't caught using any sophisticated technology, though—he was caught because he bragged about his hacking exploits to one too many friends!

Remember what I said earlier about how teenagers struggle to keep private information from going public? This young person shared a bit too much, and his bragging landed him in jail because his pride won out.

It's easy for online communication to become all you know. You become so popular online and in knowing how to communicate online that you forget how to communicate in the real world.

This just pulls you in farther.

A good example of this is when you are having a meal with your friends or family. Do you spend time together making eye contact and conversing . . . or is everyone constantly looking at their screens? Not being able to communicate appropriately in the real world will eventually be a big setback in your life.

// REBELLION

Rebellion isn't a cool word. It isn't popular, and no one really wants to hear it . . . and I understand no one really wants to read it either. Unless of course you are part of the Rebel Alliance in Star Wars. Unfortunately, rebellion is part of our lives at all ages, and it needs to be understood. For some, being called a rebel is cool. For others, it represents a life separated from God.

The simplest definition of rebellion is to resist authority. If our goal is to live under Christ, then rebelling against Him doesn't line up. Rebellion can take many shapes. Sometimes it is not doing what your parents ask you to do. Other times it might be disobeying the speed limit. Rebellion is not limited by technology; rebellion actually thrives because of it.

Rebellion is another draw to online communication. We receive positive affirmation through likes and positive comments, but if someone disagrees with what we're saying or challenges us, it is easy to rebel against them and ignore their point by tuning them out.

In the real world, if someone is pressuring us to do something wrong (or something right!), we have to interact with him or her at some level. We have to confront the person with words or place a physical distance between us. But online, I can just block them and disappear.

Online, if I don't like what you're telling me, whether good or bad, I can easily escape. I can stop messaging you, and then I can block you from all forms of communication with me. Instead of listening to your side of an argument and possibly changing my perspective because of what you shared, I can delete your comment or type back a mean comment. Sometimes, my friends who agree with me will comment in my defense, and this supports my position even more. If you tell me to do something I don't want to do, it is easy to get away from that. Social media can be an echo chamber that reassures your current views and never challenges you to change. This can lead to defying authority and a lack of respect for others.

// ACCEPTANCE

We all have a desire to be accepted, which is a driving force behind many of our actions today. From the time we're infants and through adulthood, we all want to be approved. We want to be able to communicate. When you were a baby, you figured this out pretty quickly. What did you do when you were hungry or your diaper was dirty? You cried. I cried. We all cried out to get attention and approval because we wanted to be accepted. Social media can be a way we cry out for approval and gain acceptance.

And it works both ways—you look for approval, but you can also give it (or not give it!). Social media allows you to communicate instantly with the masses. That's a scary concept. With a few clicks, you can very easily build people up or tear them down. You can encourage someone or destroy someone. You can influence the kingdom of heaven or you can support the kingdom of earth. That is a lot of power when you think about it.

You also have a lot of power when it comes to the next big thing in technology. By deciding to use Instagram, you made it worth $1 billion to Facebook. *You* gave Facebook its start. This cycle continues as new sites and apps come out, and teens as a group have the power to make or break them. Once your parents figure out each app, you usually move on to the next thing—which in and of itself isn't a bad thing. It's your motives that count. Staying ahead with new apps so you can keep hiding your online activities from your parents *is* a bad thing—it's not a Christ-like way to handle this part of your life.

// SO WHAT'S THE BIG DEAL?

All of this—seeking pride, popularity, acceptance, and reassurance through social media—can lead to ranking God second or third place in our lives. Especially when we are seeking to fill these needs through social media instead of through Him! It's a problem when family communication takes a backseat, and a desire to always be online goes above and beyond any other expectations that may be placed on us.

In that case, the internet becomes an idol. It becomes something we worship. We may not physically bow down to it, but we might as well. Do you want anyone seeing you on your knees bowing to your cell phone? Unlikely. Then consider your actions and what they communicate you are worshiping—and who.

The advertising world has taken notice of this development in our culture. You can find commercials for macaroni and cheese where the tagline is that the mac and cheese is so good it will make you put down your phone and actually eat dinner with your parents. A paper plate commercial is based on the concept that it's important for you to put your phone down and have a meal with friends without worrying about who will do the dishes.

Even our country is trying to figure out how to handle the issues young people create online. Bully laws are being passed in many states because bullies are moving online, taking their real-world behavior with them.

So where does this leave us?

Whose problem is this, after all?

Is it social media's fault?

Is it your fault?

Is it your parents' fault?

It won't help us to blame a certain social media site, or even the internet in general. They provide services that require responsibility to use. Matthew 7:3 says, "And why worry about a speck in your friend's eye when you have a log in your own?"

While I agree that there are problems with social media sites, I don't believe it is their job to help us become more like Christ. You have to own that one yourself.

How could a social networking website apply Matthew 5:16 that says, "In the same way, let your good deeds shine out for all to see, so that everyone will praise your heavenly Father"? Social media can't do this by itself. **We need to let Christ's light shine in the way *we* use the technology that's available to us.**

PART THREE:

How To Unhook

If the Bible is the standard by which we live and to which we hold ourselves, then **how does that affect what you put on the internet and what you are texting your friends?** Ask yourself these questions about what you are posting:

1. How does my use of technology help people glorify God?

2. Is the content shining God's light in a dark world?

I am very pro-technology and pro-social media, but like most things in life, you have to earn the privilege to use it and then continue to use it responsibly. For example, when you learn to drive, you don't get behind the wheel of a racecar at the Indianapolis 500 right away. You start by going one mile per hour in a parking lot with your parent freaked out in the passenger seat—and you move up from there. We have to earn the privilege to use social media and then work hard to use that privilege responsibly.

Here are some tools to success.

// OBEY BOUNDARIES

Do you believe your parents are looking out for your best interest? If your parents have some boundaries on your online activities, chances are, they are trying to help you. Does the Bible say you have to obey your parents only if they know more about something than you do? In case you were wondering . . . no, it does not. It says you are to obey them. Ephesians 6:1 says, "Children, obey your parents because you belong to the Lord, for this is the right thing to do."

It doesn't say to obey only if it makes sense, or to obey only if you like it. The Bible says to obey. Mastering this concept now will definitely help you later in life if you ever have an unreasonable boss. But let's keep reading in Ephesians. Verse 2 says you are to "'Honor your father and mother.' This is the first commandment with a promise." Obedience to your parents is so important that it is one of the Ten Commandments. Think about that.

Then in verse 3 the Bible gives us that promise. It says, "If you honor your father and mother, 'things will go well for you, and you will have a long life on the earth.'" What does it say? What's that about a long life? Could it be that the Bible is telling you that obedience to your parents might increase your lifespan? It makes sense. Why do your parents tell you not to play with knives, or run with scissors, or to look both ways before crossing the street? Many of these things are to keep you safe and protect your life, which will make it longer.

This isn't a golden ticket, obviously, but the Bible is saying that the reward for obedience is peace through Christ in our lives, both when times are good and when times are hard. It is also interesting to note that the Bible has more warnings about not honoring and obeying your parents than it does blessings for honoring and obeying them. Take a minute and think about that. #heavy #deep

If your parents have set online curfews for you, obey them. If they don't want you logging in to certain social media sites, obey them. If they encourage you not to hang around with certain people online—or offline—obey them. A key evidence that you are becoming an adult is not your age or size but your ability to think like an adult and accept parental counsel.

The Bible actually commands your parents to parent you. Proverbs 22:6 tells your parents, "Direct your children onto the right path, and when they are older, they will not leave it." In Ephesians 6:4, the rest of the passage we were reading earlier, it says, "Fathers, do not provoke your children to anger by the way you treat them. Rather, bring them up with the discipline and instruction that comes from the Lord."

Remember, *parents* refers to the authority that God has placed over you at this time in your life. That may be parents in the traditional sense, or it may be parents in the nontraditional sense, referring to your grandparents, other family members, foster parents, or whomever God has placed as an authority over you at this stage of your life. **The Bible applies to any and all life situations.**

Our legal system is also trying to help set boundaries. Texting and driving is a deadly epidemic. *Texting and driving* does not just mean sending texts, it refers to anything taking your attention away from driving by using your device. In the context of driving, the government is trying to set some boundaries for us to obey. While many states have texting-and-driving laws, it is almost universally agreed upon that they are difficult to enforce. I don't want my kids killing someone with the car because they were using the internet while driving. **Show some restraint and maturity. Uphold the law, and uphold your parents' boundaries.** Otherwise, it's not only your life that may be in danger, but also someone else's.

// SEEK OUT GODLY RELATIONSHIPS

Do your friends model a godly example? Do they encourage you to become more like Christ, or are they encouraging you to be more and more like the world? One scary statistic is that over 80% of you who

IT IS IMPORTANT TO SURROUND OURSELVES WITH GODLY FRIENDS

join a social media website do so at the encouragement of your friends. It gets even more extreme when you consider that the same statistic applies to those who view pornography online. It is one thing to join a social network because your friends joined; it is another thing to sin with pornography.

The above statistic tells us that we are very open to suggestions, and we often follow them. That's human nature, and **that's why it is important to surround ourselves with godly friends.** Remember those boundaries we talked about? What happens when you are at a friend's house and away from your parents' restrictions? Are you encouraged to honor your parents, or to go a different way?

Proverbs 27:17 says, "As iron sharpens iron, so a friend sharpens a friend." Do your friends sharpen you and encourage you to be more like Christ, both in the real world and in the virtual world of social media?

Proverbs 18:24 says, "A man of too many friends comes to ruin, but there is a friend who sticks closer than a brother" (NASB). I love this verse. It was written over 900 years before Christ was born, long before the internet was even a gleam in anyone's eye, long before Facebook friends were even a thing. Latch on to what it says, though—too many friends can bring you to ruin. Do you even know who your "friends" are online? Do you take great pride in how many friends and followers you have? Should you? Ask yourself, do you have the one and only friend who sticks closer than a brother?

I love that the Bible is applicable to all areas of life. **Social media didn't surprise God.** Unlike the fads of social media with sites and apps that come and go, the Bible is timeless. God wrote His book to help us with all areas of our lives. Whether someone is living now or will be living 1000 years from now, the Bible will still be the only source of truth and the only way to heaven.

// BE RESPONSIBLE

Did you know that internet use is not an inalienable right? It is not guaranteed. The Bible says that your parents have to care for you with food, clothing, and shelter—but it does not say they have to provide you with internet access, smartphones, and cool gadgets. Using the internet and your smartphone is a privilege that is earned through responsibility, regardless of who is paying for it. I pay for my own cell phone and internet access, but that doesn't mean the Bible no longer applies to me.

The same is true with driving. The government is happy to issue you a driver's license and allow you to drive a motor vehicle . . . as long as you are responsible and obey the laws. Disobey those laws or act irresponsibly on the road, and not only will you be fined and even put in jail, but the authorities can also revoke your driving privileges completely by taking back your driver's license.

My children know that the privilege to use their iPads and our internet service—which my wife and I pay for—can be revoked at any time if they are not used responsibly. I would encourage your parents to do the same thing. If you aren't responsible, your devices and internet access should all be removed. **While that may not be convenient for you or your parents, encouraging you to be godly shouldn't be subject to convenience.**

When I was a kid, a pastor at my church called this kind of thing "radical amputation," by which he meant, "Get the sin out of your life!" While that sounds drastic, this is how important it is that we do whatever it takes to live a life that honors Christ. Would you be willing to radically remove your device from your life if that would help you become more like Christ?

Despite our super-connected world, you don't *have* to be connected to live. You need food to live, and water—but not internet access, not social media. If social media is causing you to sin, then it should be removed from your life. Actually, the best thing for you might be to switch back to a plain old dumb phone if it helps you become more like Christ.

In 1 Corinthians 10:31 we read, "So whether you eat or drink, or whatever you do [post online, or lurk, or browse the internet], do it all for the glory of God."

Can that be said of you?

Colossians 3:23–24 says, "Work willingly at whatever you do, as though you were working for the Lord rather than for people. Remember that the Lord will give you an inheritance as your reward, and that the Master you are serving is Christ."

Do you get that? **You don't do things for anyone other than the Lord.** Not for men, but for Jesus. Why? Because while you may get some rewards here on earth, those are temporary—they don't last for very long. But the rewards from Jesus in heaven last forever. Which would you prefer? As a teenager it may seem as if life will last a long time . . . but trust me, it won't. It will be over before you know it.

Remember, eternity is a long time. Even if you live 100 years, you can't take anything on earth with you. You never see a hearse pulling a U-Haul, taking the dead's belongings along to the cemetery. Really, 100 years is nothing compared to eternity, even though it may seem like a long time now.

So, if you admit that you are struggling with being responsible with your usage of social media, how do you make changes? The Bible has the answer. Ephesians 4:22–24 tells us how. "Throw off your old sinful nature and your former way of life, which is corrupted by lust and deception. Instead, let the Spirit renew your thoughts and attitudes. Put on your new nature, created to be like God—truly righteous and holy."

First, you have to **throw or put off**. So, in the case of online gossip, you have to put off gossip. In other words, don't do it.

Second, and most importantly, **you have to use the power of the Holy Spirit to renew or change your thinking**. It isn't just enough to stop gossiping—you have to change to understand that gossip is a sin and God hates sin. Otherwise, if you just stop without renewing your mind, you are still a gossip; you are just hiding it better.

Third, you have to **put on your new nature**. So, instead of gossiping, you encourage and lift up other people. You build up, instead of tearing down. You also confront other people who gossip after you've changed and know that it is a sin.

When is a thief no longer a thief? It isn't when he stops stealing, but rather when he stops stealing and changes his heart and then gets a job to support himself. Change is hard, but if you follow these three steps—**put off, renew, and put on**—then, with the help of the Holy Spirit, you can change and continue to grow in responsibility in all areas of life.

// BE ACCOUNTABLE

The Bible says in Romans 14:12, "Yes, each of us will give a personal account to God." This means that we will give an account to God for everything we do during this life on earth. Whether in the real world or the virtual world, we will all give an account. While that may sound scary, it isn't if we **view it as a motivation to do what's right.**

Which is better? Learning about using technology and social media from your parents so that you are using it in a Christ-honoring fashion? Or establishing bad habits now because you are rebelling against your parents' authority, which will create a lot for you to give an account for later?

Auto insurance companies have even figured this out. They now provide technology you can plug into your car so your parents can see how you're driving. If you're a safe, responsible driver, then your parents save money on your car insurance, but if you're a dangerous and reckless driver, then your parents pay more. Or maybe, *you* pay more. Either way, the day of reckoning or accountability with the insurance company is pretty quick. Not all accountability is as instant.

The question is, are you willing to be held accountable and have your parents, teachers, youth workers, and pastors help you? How many social media accounts do you want to give an account for? **A study by CNN showed that parental involvement "effectively erased the negative effects" of social media on their kids.** That's not the Bible saying your parents' involvement is good for you, that's a study by CNN! **It just so happens that the Bible says the same thing.**

Are you willing to submit to your parents' authority and allow them to hold you accountable? How will that look in your life? I'm so glad you asked. Here are some suggestions.

1. Be up-front with your logs and history. Don't try to hide it or erase where you go and what you do online.

2. Make sure your parents know your passwords to all your accounts.

3. Friend your parents online.

4. Offer to help your parents learn about the latest social media fads during family time.

5. Suggest software for filtering or tracking.

6. Tell your parents where you get online.

7. When you goof, own it. Admit to it. Change and grow. Don't use your superior knowledge as an excuse not to learn from your mistakes or to hide them.

It's much better to humble yourself and learn now than to spend decades addicted to your screen because you thought you were too smart to ask for help or admit your mistakes. That kind of pride can lead to other screen-related addictions, like pornography.

There is also a level of security when you are under your parents' umbrella of accountability. If you obey them, then you are accountable only for your own obedience; they are accountable for what they've told you to do. However, when you disobey them and go out on your own, you remove their protective umbrella—and you become directly accountable before God. Don't miss out on that protection as a young person just because you think you know more than they do. Eventually, as you grow into an adult, that protection goes away because your relationship with your parents changes from an authoritative one to that of an advisor. Sometimes I wish I were you.

PART FOUR:

Challenges

Now that you know some of the reasons that social media draws us in, and you understand the importance of submitting your social media use to Christ, here are some practical ways to obey your parents' rules, seek out godly relationships, act responsibly, and be accountable.

1. Keep a log of all your social media activity for a day/week and review it with your parents.

2. Be uplifting and not self-promoting online.

3. Unfollow those who don't help you become more like Christ.

4. Make a list of all the locations where you get online (school, the library, a friend's house, coffee shops…) and share it with your parents.

5. Make sure you aren't spending more time on social media than studying the Bible.

6. Take initiative and put down your device at dinner and during family time.

7. Post one item per day that encourages others and helps them become more like Christ.

We will all be judged for our actions. I think we tend to forget what *all* means and that it applies to each one of us. **We are accountable for our own actions both in the real world and in the online world.** Parents are accountable for their children, and you are accountable for yourself before God. God is still God, even online.